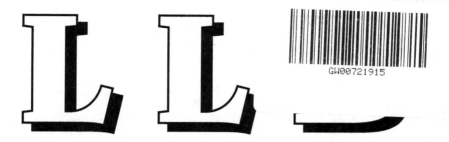

LAW OF TRUSTS
Suggested Solutions

UNIVERSITY OF LONDON
June Examination 1991

HLT Publications

HLT PUBLICATIONS
200 Greyhound Road, London W14 9RY

Examination Questions © The University of London 1991
Solutions © The HLT Group Ltd 1991

ISBN 1 85352 978 8

British Library Cataloguing-in-Publication.

A CIP Catalogue record for this book is available from the
British Library.

Printed and bound in Great Britain.

Contents

Acknowledgement

The questions used are taken from past University of London LLB (External) Degree examination papers and our thanks are extended to the University of London for the kind permission which has been given to us to use and publish the questions.

Caveat:

The answers given are not approved or sanctioned by the University of London and are entirely our responsibility.

They are not intended as 'Model Answers', but rather as Suggested Solutions.

The answers have two fundamental purposes, namely:

a) To provide a detailed example of a suggested solution to examination questions, and

b) To assist students with their research into the subject and to further their understanding and appreciation of the subject of Laws.

Note:

Please note that the solutions in this book were written in the year of the examination for each paper. They were appropriate solutions at the time of preparation, but students must note that certain caselaw and statutes may subsequently have changed.

Introduction

Why choose HLT publications

Holborn College has earned an International reputation over the past ten years for the outstanding quality of its teaching, Textbooks, Casebooks and Suggested Solutions to past examination papers set by the various examining bodies.

Our expertise is reflected in the outstanding results achieved by our students in the examinations conducted by the University of London, the Law Society, the Council of Legal Education and the Associated Examining Board.

The object of Suggested Solutions

The Suggested Solutions have been prepared by College lecturers experienced in teaching to this specific syllabus and are intended to be an example of a full answer to the problems posed by the examiner.

They are not 'model answers', for at this level there almost certainly is not just one answer to a problem, nor are the answers written to strict examination time limits.

The opportunity has been taken, where appropriate, to develop themes, suggest alternatives and set out additional material to an extent not possible by the examinee in the examination room.

We feel that in writing full opinion answers to the questions that we can assist you with your research into the subject and can further your understanding and appreciation of the law.

Notes on examination technique

Although the SUBSTANCE and SLANT of the answer changes according to the subject-matter of the question, the examining body and syllabus concerned, the TECHNIQUE of answering examination questions does not change.

You will not pass an examination if you do not know the substance of a course. You may pass if you do not know how to go about answering a question although this is doubtful. To do well and to guarantee success, however, it is necessary to learn the technique of answering problems properly. The following is a guide to acquiring that technique.

1 *Time*

All examinations permit only a limited time for papers to be completed. All papers require you to answer a certain number of questions in that time, and the questions, with some exceptions carry equal marks.

It follows from this that you should never spend a disproportionate amount of time on any question. When you have used up the amount of time allowed for any one question STOP and go on to the next question after an abrupt conclusion, if necessary. If you feel that you are running out of time, then complete your answer in *note form*. A useful way of ensuring that you do not over-run is to write down on a piece of scrap paper the time at which you should be starting each part of the paper. This can be done in the few minutes before the examination begins and it will help you to calm any nerves you may have.

2 *Reading the question*

It will not be often that you will be able to answer every question on an examination paper. Inevitably, there will be some areas in which you feel better prepared than others. You will prefer to answer the questions which deal with those areas, but you will never know how good the questions are *unless you read the whole examination paper*.

You should spend *at least* 10 MINUTES at the beginning of the examination reading the questions. Preferably, you should read them more than once. As you go through each question, make a brief note on the examination paper of any relevant cases and/or statutes that occur to you even if you think you may not answer that question: you may well be grateful for this note towards the end of the examination when you are tired and your memory begins to fail.

3 *Re-reading the answers*

Ideally, you should allow time to re-read your answers. This is rarely a pleasant process, but will ensure that you do not make any silly mistakes such as leaving out a 'not' when the negative is vital.

4 *The structure of the answer*

Almost all examination problems raise more than one legal issue that you are required to deal with. Your answer should:

i) *identify the issues raised by the question*

This is of crucial importance and gives shape to the whole answer. It indicates to the examiner that you appreciate what he is asking you about.

This is at least as important as actually answering the questions of law raised by that issue.

The issues should be identified in the first paragraph of the answer.

ii) *deal with those issues one by one as they arise in the course of the problem*

This, of course, is the substance of the answer and where study and revision pays off.

iii) *if the answer to an issue turns on a provision of a statute, CITE that provision briefly, but do not quote it from any statute you may be permitted to bring into the examination hall*

Having cited the provision, show how it is relevant to the question.

iv) *if there is no statute, or the meaning of the statute has been interpreted by the courts, CITE the relevant cases*

'Citing cases' does not mean writing down the nature of every case that happens to deal with the general topic with which you are concerned and then detailing all the facts you can think of.

You should cite *only* the most relevant cases - there may perhaps only be one. No more facts should be stated than are absolutely essential to establish the relevance of the case. If there is a relevant case, but you cannot remember its name, it is sufficient to refer to it as 'one decided case'.

v) *whenever a statute or case is cited, the title of statute or the name of the case should be underlined*

This makes the examiner's job much easier because he can see at a glance whether the relevant material has been dealt with, and it will make him more disposed in your favour.

vi) *having dealt with the relevant issues, summarise your conclusions in such a way that you answer the question*

A question will often say at the end simply 'Advise A', or B, or C, etc. The advice will usually turn on the individual answers to a number of issues. The point made here is that the final paragraph should pull those individual answers together *and actually give the advice required.* For example, it may begin something like: 'The effect of the answer to the issues raised by this question is that one's advice to A is that ...'

vii) *related to (vi), make sure at the end that you have answered the question*

For example, if the question says 'Advise A', make sure that is what your answer does. If you are required to advise more than one party, make sure that you have dealt with all the parties that you are required to and no more.

5 *Some general points*

You should always try to get the examiner on your side. One method has already been mentioned - the underlining of case names, etc. There are also other ways as well.

Always write as *neatly* as you can. This is more easily done with ink than with a ball-point.

Avoid the use of violently coloured ink eg turquoise; this makes a paper difficult to read.

Space out your answers sensibly: leave a line between paragraphs. You can always get more paper. At the same time, try not to use so much paper that your answer book looks too formidable to mark. This is a question of personal judgment.

NEVER put in irrelevant material simply to show that you are clever. Irrelevance is not a virtue and time spent on it is time lost for other, relevant, answers.

EXAMINATION PAPER

UNIVERSITY OF LONDON
LLB EXAMINATION
PART I for External Students

LAW OF TRUSTS

Wednesday, 5 June 1991: 10 am to 1 pm

Answer four of the following eight questions

1.   a)   Distinguish between wholly secret and half-secret trusts. Is there any, and if so what, *rationale* for the different 'communication' rules?

     b)   By his will, a testator left £50,000 to A and B and added 'it being my wish that they will give effect to the purposes set out in a separate letter which I have signed and handed to B'. Before the will was made, the testator revealed the contents of the letter to A alone, and then sealed it and handed it over to B saying that it was only to be opened after his death.

          Following the testator's death earlier this year, B opened the letter and found that it contained a direction to A and B to pay the £50,000 to the testator's former secretary, C who, one week before the testator's death, was killed in a car accident leaving an infant daughter, D.

          Advise A and B as to what they should do with the £50,000.

2.   'Purpose trusts are either charitable or non-charitable. If they are charitable, they are free from many constraints which apply to private trusts and, if they are non-charitable, they are subject to constraints from which other private trusts are free.'

     Develop and illustrate this proposition by reference to the relevant authorities.

3.   a)   'Constructive trusts show the conscience of equity at work.'

          Discuss.

     b)   Jack and Jill have for the last two years been living together in a flat. Jill had been the tenant of the flat for several years when, last year, the landlord offered to grant a 99-year lease to Jill at a nominal rent for £20,000, a price that was low by reason of the fact that Jill was a protected sitting tenant. Jill agreed but at her request the 99-year lease was granted to Jack who provided the whole of the £20,000. On the open market and with vacant possession, the leasehold flat would fetch £40,000 and Jack, having become disenchanted with Jill, is talking of selling and keeping the entire proceeds.

Advise Jill as to her interest, if any, in the flat or its future proceeds, on the assumption that her tenancy came to an end when Jack purchased.

4. By her will, Celia, after appointing Tug and Tow to be her executors and trustees, left her residuary estate to them upon trust to divide it into two equal parts and to hold such parts upon the following trusts:

   a) As to one part, upon trust to pay the income thereof to her husband, Henry, for life upon protective trusts and subject thereto upon trust for such of her children as should attain the age of 25;

   b) As to the other part, upon trust in equal shares for such of her children as should be living when her youngest child attains the age of 18.

Celia died last year leaving Henry and three children surviving, Tom, Dick, and Harriet, aged 3, 14 and 21.

Advise Tug and Tow:

   i) Whether they may have recourse to the trust income of either fund to pay school fees for Dick;

   ii) Whether they may apply trust capital from either fund to enable Harriet to purchase a fast food franchise (a business in which she has five years' experience);

   iii) Pending the attainment by Tom of the age of 18, what they should do with the income of fund b);

   iv) In the event of Henry's bankruptcy, what they should do with the income of fund a).

5. By a settlement made by Smith, the trustees, Dum and Dee, were directed to hold a trust fund consisting of shares and debentures in

Alpha plc, a public limited company, and certain government stock, on trust to pay the income to Adam for life remainder to his children. The settlement contains no special investment clause except a provision that, before making any change of investment, the trustees should first obtain the consent in writing of Smith.

In 1987, Dum and Dee, with the consent in writing of Smith, sold the shares in Alpha to one of themselves, Dum, for £200,000 (their quoted value) and invested the proceeds in the purchase of shares in Beta plc, another public limited company.

In 1988, Dum and Dee, with the consent in writing of Smith, sold the government stock for £500,000 (its quoted value) and invested the proceeds in the purchase of freehold offices in Docklands.

In 1989, Dum and Dee, without the consent of Smith but with the encouragement of Adam, sold the debentures in Alpha plc for £100,000 (their market value) and invested the proceeds in shares in Delta plc, another public limited company.

The shares in Alpha plc are now worth £300,000; the shares in Beta plc are now worth £100,000; the shares in Delta plc are now worth £200,000 and the freehold offices are worth £250,000.

Advise a) Adam's children, b) Dum and Dee jointly as trustees, and c) Dum individually, as to their respective legal positions.

6. a) In what circumstances may a trustee be remunerated for his services to the trust?

    b) Consider the application of the maxim *delegatus non potest delegare* in the context of a trustee of a personalty settlement who wishes:

    i) to go abroad for a period which may be between six to eighteen months;

    ii) to delegate to a stockbroker the power at his discretion to make changes of investment with a view to producing balanced gains in capital and income;

    iii) in exercise of an express power to revoke the trusts of the settlement and declare other trusts for the benefit of all or any of the same beneficiaries, to vest part of the trust fund in other trustees upon discretionary trusts for the beneficiaries.

7. Under the terms of the will of a testator who died in 1983, a fund of £3,000,000 was left to trustees upon trust to distribute the capital amongst such charitable or worthy causes and in such shares as the trustees should in their absolute discretion think fit and the residuary estate was left to the XY Charity. On various dates since the testator's death, the trustees dealt with the fund as follows:

   i) £1m was paid to the AB hospital which spent £500,000 on dialysis machines and computer equipment and invested the balance in government stock which is now worth £550,000;

   ii) £1m was paid to the CD University which applied the money towards the cost of a new library building. The total cost of the building was £2m;

   iii) £1m was paid to the EF Foundation for the Relief of Poverty. It paid this sum into its bank account which at the time was £200,000 in credit. The following day, the EF Foundation drew out £500,000 and applied it in providing hotel accommodation for the homeless. One week later, it received a donation of £500,000 and paid this sum into its account. Since then, further sums have been drawn out and the present credit balance is £400,000.

   Advise the XY Charity.

8. a) In what circumstances, if any, may the administration of an English trust be transferred abroad (in the sense of the trust fund being invested in overseas investments and the trustees being non-UK residents)?

   b) Under the terms of a settlement, investments worth £500,000 are held upon trust to hold the income on protective trusts for Mary during her life and subject thereto for such of her children as attain the age of 21 in equal shares.

   Mary is a widow aged 50 and has three children aged 18, 20 and 23. Mary and her children are all agreed that they would like to terminate the trust and divide the investments amongst themselves in agreed shares.

   Consider whether this may be done i) without an application to the court, and ii) by making such an application.

SUGGESTED SOLUTIONS

Question 1

a) Distinguish between wholly secret and half-secret trusts. Is there any, and if so what, *rationale* for the different 'communication' rules?

b) By his will, a testator left £50,000 to A and B and added 'it being my wish that they will give effect to the purposes set out in a separate letter which I have signed and handed to B'. Before the will was made, the testator revealed the contents of the letter to A alone, and then sealed it and handed it over to B saying that it was only to be opened after his death.

Following the testator's death earlier this year, B opened the letter and found that it contained a direction to A and B to pay the £50,000 to the testator's former secretary, C who, one week before the testator's death, was killed in a car accident leaving an infant daughter, D.

Advise A and B as to what they should do with the £50,000.

Suggested Solution to Question 1

General comment
This is a fairly standard question on the law relating to secret trusts. An explanation of the rationale for secret trusts will help explain the answers to the practical problems the examiner has devised in part b). A good question to answer as the law on secret trusts is usually self-contained.

Skeleton solution
Explain the difference between wholly secret and half-secret trusts – emphasise the communication rules – the 'evidence' theory – the 'incorporation' theory – Time of creation of secret trusts – possibility of revocation – *Re Gardner*.

Suggested solution
a) According to Pennycuick J in *Re Tyler*, the 'particular principles of law applicable to secret trusts are really concerned only with trusts created by will' and it is by construing the terms of a will that the most obvious difference between wholly and half secret trusts can be seen. Wholly secret trusts are those which according to the terms of the will are expressed as an absolute gift to a legatee, but where during the lifetime of the testator (before or after the making of his will) he has indicated to the legatee that the gift is to be held on trust for another person. Half secret trusts occur where the testator has left property by will 'on trust' to a legatee but where the will does not identify the terms of the trust or the intended beneficiary. In the case of half-secret trusts, the communication and acceptance of the trust and its terms must be made 'before or at the time of' the making of the will (*Re Keen*), and not afterwards. It also appears from *Re Keen* that in half secret trusts (but possibly not wholly secret), the communication to the trustee must not contradict the explicit terms of the will. Other differences are first, that wholly secret trusts of land do not need to comply with s53(1)(b) of the Law of Property Act 1925 (*Ottaway v Norman*), but half secret trusts of land do (*Re Baillie*), although the latter case may well be wrong on the ground that 'equity will not permit a statute (s53) to be an instrument of fraud'; secondly, that in half-secret trusts, gifts to two or more trustees will be to them as joint tenants and therefore an acceptance by any one of them of the trust

before the will is made will bind them all (*Re Stead*), but that in wholly secret trusts the gift *may* be to them as tenants in common so that only those who actually accept are bound; and thirdly, whereas a wholly secret trust can be revoked and replaced by a new wholly secret trust by the testator at any time up to his death, a half secret trust can only be revoked and the property held on resulting trust (because it is impossible to communicate a new trust after the will has been written).

The major difference is the communication rule, although there does not seem to be any satisfactory explanation for its existence. Indeed, in some common law jurisdictions (eg Australia) the distinction has been abolished and the wholly secret trust rule applied to both types. Two of the more cogent theories are: first, that the rule allowing acceptance after the will in wholly secret trusts was originally procedural viz, that evidence of events occurring after the will (ie acceptance) could be admitted by a court to prove a wholly secret trust so as to prevent fraud by the legatee/trustee. The fraud being that the legatee might otherwise keep property which he has promised to pass to someone else. But, in half-secret trusts, where the legatee is clearly stated to be a trustee, there is no possibility of fraud and therefore no need to examine the events occurring (ie acceptance) after the will was signed. Hence, acceptance after the will was not relevant. In other words, a rule of evidence has turned into a substantive rule of law; secondly, it may be that the half secret trust rule is a ghastly mistake because of confusion with the law of incorporation of documents. A will may be said to 'incorporate' another document if the will makes reference to that document *and* if that document was in existence at the time the will was made. It is easy to see how this rule could have been carried over to require acceptance of the trust at the time the will was made for half secret trusts. Of course, it is clear that neither of these theories (nor any other) is wholly satisfactory and the distinction should be abolished.

b) The immediate question to answer here is whether this is a wholly secret or fully secret trust. The crucial words are 'it being my wish'. If this imposes an obligation on A and B, it is half secret; if not, the words are to be ignored and we must consider the law of wholly secret trusts. These are precatory words and, following *Lambe* v *Eames*, they do not readily impose a trust. However, this is a marginal case — .

though more likely fully secret – and the better student will deal with both alternatives.

i) If half secret – there must be communication and acceptance before or at the time of the will and this has clearly been the case with A. The gift will be to them as joint tenants (because they are trustees), so A's acceptance will bind B (*Re Stead*). Note, however, that B has in any event accepted the terms of the trust before the will by accepting a sealed envelope containing those details before the will was made – *Re Keen, Re Boyes* ('a ship sailing under sealed orders'). The trust is therefore prima facie valid and neither A nor B can keep the money. However, whether they hand it on to the beneficiary (C and hence D) or whether it results to the testator's next of kin depends on whether it matters that the intended beneficiary (C) died before the testator. *Re Gardner (No 2)* says that the estate of a beneficiary obtains their intended interest under a half secret trust even if that beneficiary dies before the testator. However, this may be wrong as it appears that secret trusts do not come into existence until the testator dies and, therefore, people who die before him are not really beneficiaries – they have no interest when they die. If *Re Gardner* is wrong, the money results to the next of kin and not C's estate (D).

ii) If fully secret – the date of communication is irrelevant so long as it is before the testator's death. Given that A (directly) and B (by means of accepting the envelope) have both accepted the trust it is irrelevant whether the gift to them was as joint tenants or tenants in common. They are both bound. Hence the question is the same as above viz, whether *Re Gardner No 2* is correct. In the case of fully secret trusts, it is rather more certain that the trust does not arise until the testator's death and therefore anybody who dies before him can have no claim. The money goes to the testator's next of kin.

Question 2

'Purpose trusts are either charitable or non-charitable. If they are charitable, they are free from many constraints which apply to private trusts and, if they are non-charitable, they are subject to constraints from which other private trusts are free.'

Develop and illustrate this proposition by reference to the relevant authorities.

Suggested Solution to Question 2

General comment

This is a cleverly worded question and many students will fall into the trap of simply describing the 'beneficiary principle' and/or the law of charities. However, the question asks about the consequence of something being charitable or non-charitable rather than how the law defines those categories. It requires good knowledge of both areas of the law and is an object lesson in why a student should never omit these topics from her or his revision.

Skeleton solution

Definition of purpose trusts – essential invalidity contrasted with essential validity of charities – Perpetuity rule – problems of enforcement – tax benefits – trustee's powers – use of cy-près.

Suggested solution

Normally trusts must have certain objects (*Re Endacott*). Generally, this means that a trust must either be for the benefit of human beneficiaries (*Re Astor*) or fall within the definition of charity. To the first rule (the need for human beneficiaries), there are only limited exceptions – sometimes known as the anomalous exceptions of *Re Endacott* or 'trusts of imperfect obligation' viz, trusts for the erection and maintenance of monuments and graves (*Re Gibson not Re Hetherington* or *Bourne* v *Keane* or *Re Caius*), trusts for the maintenance of specific animals (*Re Dean*) and the trusts in *Re Thompson* for the promotion of fox-hunting. Reference must also be made to the rule in *Re Denley*, that only those non-charitable purpose trusts that are 'abstract or impersonal' are void and, therefore, a trust which 'directly or indirectly' benefits ascertainable individuals may still be valid. However, herein lies the first and foremost distinction between charitable and non-charitable purpose trusts – the former are valid, the great majority of the latter are void. This is the greatest 'constraint' to which non-charitable purpose trusts are subject and which obviously does not apply to charitable purpose trusts or private trusts which have a human beneficiary.

a) *Valid non-charitable purpose trusts and private trusts*

The major difference between these two types of trust is that valid non-charitable purpose trusts (*Endacott* exceptions and *Re Denley*) have difficulty satisfying the perpetuity rule. To be valid, these purpose trusts must not last longer than the perpetuity period ie, they can exist only for a certain maximum duration. This is often expressed as 'the rule against perpetual trusts'. This perpetuity period is 'a life in being plus twenty-one years' ie the length of the life of any person named in the document establishing the trust plus 21 years after their death. However, because these trusts are normally established by will, the 'life in being' is usually the testator (now dead) and therefore the period is only 21 years. It seems that such a trust satisfies the perpetuity period only if it is possible to say at the outset that it will definitely not last longer than the perpetuity period, which means in effect that the will or deed must contain a clause such as 'for so long as the law allows' or 'for 21 years' or 'for the perpetuity period' – *Leahy* v *AG for New South Wales*; *Re Denley*. (NB *Re Drummond* gives a different test viz, whether the capital sum could be spent within the period, but this is probably not correct). This is a difficult test to satisfy and certainly is a 'constraint' on the validity of such trusts. Pure private trusts (those with a human beneficiary) usually have no difficulty meeting this test and, in any event, have the benefit of the Perpetuities and Accumulations Act 1964. Valid purpose trusts cannot rely on the provisions of this Act to save what would otherwise be void for perpetuity under the common law – s15(4) PAA 1964. It is also clear (at least for the *Endacott* exceptions), that valid purpose trusts suffer from problems of enforcement – there is no beneficiary who has an interest to go to court to compel the trustees to carry out the trust. This is why these trusts are known as 'trusts of imperfect obligation' – because the trustee's obligation is imperfect. This is often circumvented by giving the residuary legatees of the will (if any) the power (but not the duty) to apply to the court to enforce the trust. But, this is obviously unsatisfactory because such residuary legatees would be entitled to the capital sum if the trust did fail and, therefore, it is not in their interest to see the trust performed. In pure private trusts, there is a beneficiary both capable and willing to ensure that the trustees carry out their duties.

b) *Charitable trusts and private trusts*
It is often said that the main difference between private trusts and charitable trusts is that the former must have certainty of objects whilst the latter does not. This is not strictly true. Private trusts must satisfy the certainty of objects rule by having human beneficiaries – *Re Astor*.

Charities, however, need not satisfy this rule, but must satisfy a much less stringent certainty of objects rule viz, they must fall within the category of purposes recognised by the law as charitable. This is the purpose of the *Pemsel* categories of aged, impotent, infirm; advancement of religion; advancement of education; and other purposes beneficial to the community. So, to be charitable a trust must satisfy an 'objects test' even though one less stringent than private trusts. Other advantages enjoyed by charitable trusts over private trusts are first, that charities are not subject to the perpetuity rule – they can last for ever; secondly, that charitable trusts are exempt from many taxes, rates and excise duties – the fiscal advantages which are worth about 660 million pounds a year (1991); thirdly, that charitable trustees can act by majority vote, whereas private trustees must usually act unanimously; and fourthly, that surplus assets of charitable trusts fall under the cy-pres doctrine whereas private trusts are governed by the law of resulting trusts. Charities are, however, subject to one constraint not placed upon private trusts viz, that charities must be for the public benefit. So, for charities, the purpose must be generally *beneficial* to the community *and*, for every charity except those for the relief of the poor, must benefit the public at large (or a section thereof) – *Re Compton, Dingle* v *Turner, Re Williams.*

Question 3

a) 'Constructive trusts show the conscience of equity at work.'

Discuss.

b) Jack and Jill have for the last two years been living together in a flat. Jill had been the tenant of the flat for several years when, last year, the landlord offered to grant a 99-year lease to Jill at a nominal rent for £20,000, a price that was low by reason of the fact that Jill was a protected sitting tenant. Jill agreed but at her request the 99-year lease was granted to Jack who provided the whole of the £20,000. On the open market and with vacant possession, the leasehold flat would fetch £40,000 and Jack, having become disenchanted with Jill, is talking of selling and keeping the entire proceeds.

Advise Jill as to her interest, if any, in the flat or its future proceeds, on the assumption that her tenancy came to an end when Jack purchased.

Question 3

General comment

This is a question that invites in part (a) a general description of the meaning and scope of constructive trusts. A good question to begin with and which lends itself to a second class mark. Part (b) is straightforward case law.

Skeleton solution

Trust or remedy – America vs England – standard categories of constructive trust – *Pettit* v *Pettit* – *Lloyds Bank* v *Rosset* – relationship to resulting trusts.

Suggested solution

a) Constructive trusts are often said to be at the cutting edge of a court's equitable jurisdiction. It is true that the 'constructive trust' is perceived by many to be an all-embracing remedy which the courts may use at their discretion to remedy 'inequitable' conduct by an individual, and this is indeed reinforced by the fact that constructive trusts are exempt from the normal formalities relating to the creation and operation of trusts – see s53(2) of the Law of Property Act 1925.

However, it is also clear that there is no set meaning to the term 'constructive trust' and that the many and various situations in which they can arise may defy definition. Some jurists argue that one feature common to all cases of constructive trust is that no person can be a constructive trustee (and hence there can be no constructive trust) unless he or she is the legal owner of property at the time the court imposes the trust. Such a 'definition' would seem to rule out 'knowing assistance' cases as examples of constructive trusts (because the person knowingly assisting does not have and does not acquire legal title). Another purported distinction is between the 'English' and 'American' constructive trusts, and herein lies the heart of the issue whether 'constructive trusts show the conscience of equity at work'.

The so-called 'English' approach sees constructive trusts as substantive trusts; that is, there are beneficiaries, trustees and those trustees have substantive duties of holding and administering the trust property just as if they had been constituted trustees under an express settlement. The consequence of this theoretical approach is that the court can impose a constructive trust only in certain reasonably defined situations. This does not mean that constructive trusts are not concerned with 'conscience', but rather that equity will remedy unconscionable behaviour only if certain conditions are satisfied. Examples of such constructive trusts are the rule that a trustee must not make a profit from his trust (*Keech* v *Sandford*); the rules of knowing receipt and assistance (*Lipkin Gorman* v *Karnaple, AGIP* v *Africa*); the rule that equity will not allow a statute to be an instrument of fraud (*Rochefaucauld* v *Boustead*); the law of secret trusts (possibly – see *Ottaway* v *Norman*); the rule that a person cannot retain the benefit of a criminal act (*Davitt* v *Titcumb*); the law of mutual wills (*Re Cleaver*); and the rule that a vendor holds property on constructive trusts for a purchaser under a constructive trust, even before transfer of the property, if the contract for sale is specifically enforceable (*Lysaght* v *Edwards*). All of these are cases where the court has imposed a trust to prevent inequity, but where the law has developed a reasonable certain set of rules to establish when this has occurred.

The 'American' view, on the other hand, sees the constructive trust as a flexible 'weapon' or 'remedy' which the court may use to prevent or redress inequitable conduct in any situation at any time. It is often known as the 'remedial constructive trust'. Furthermore, not only are there little restrictions on the circumstances in which such a trust can be imposed, but also the nature of this type of constructive trust is quite different. This constructive trust is clearly not substantive; the only duty which the constructive trustee will be under will be to return the trust property to its 'rightful' owner, ie the person to whom the court thinks in all fairness it should belong. It is a method of compelling a person to return property when they have been unjustly enriched. A good example in English law is *Chase Manhattan Bank* v *Israeli-British Bank,* a case often considered under the law of tracing, but more properly regarded as one of unjust enrichment or remedial constructive trust because of the absence of any recognisable fiduciary relationship between the parties. A similar approach was gaining ground in the law of matrimonial or quasi-matrimonial property where, under the guidance of *Grant* v *Edwards*, the court adopted a flexible, result-oriented approach to ownership of property on the break-up of a stable relationship. This has been somewhat restricted by *Lloyds Bank* v *Rosset* which preferred the more defined 'English view'.

All in all then, it is true on one level to say that constructive trusts are the conscience of equity at work. Their purpose is to ensure that the legal owner of property should not unlawfully deprive another of his or her property. However, the more interesting question is how flexible this jurisdiction really is. In recent years, the courts of this country have been moving towards a more relaxed attitude to the use of constructive trusts and, in this sense, we can agree with the quotation in the question.

b) There are a number of possible answers to the question whether Jill has an interest in the flat or the proceeds of sale thereof. The first, most obvious, and clearly incorrect view is that Jill has no interest in the leasehold of the flat because legal title to the flat is in Jack's name alone. This is the presumption at law but, of course, it can be rebutted by showing that Jill has an interest by virtue of a resulting or constructive trust on the *Pettit* v *Pettit, Lloyds Bank* v *Rosset* model. It is clear, however, that no resulting trust can arise in Jill's favour because she has not contributed to the purchase price of the flat – it is purchased entirely with Jack's money. Indeed, the fact that Jack has legal title and that he alone provided the purchase money could go a long way to proving his sole ownership. However, this is unlikely because it appears that Jack is behaving inequitably and may be subject to a constructive trust in Jill's favour.

There are, perhaps two ways in which Jill could establish an interest – either of the whole or part – to the flat by virtue of a constructive trust. First, she could seek to show that there was a common intention between herself and Jack that she should have an interest in the flat plus some act of detriment by her in reliance on that promise – *Lloyds Bank* v *Rosset*. On the facts, it may be possible to deduce such a common intention from the fact that she was offered the tenancy but insisted that it be given formally to Jack. Unless this was tantamount to a gift, there is little to explain such action unless Jill did have such intention. Her detriment would be similar to that in *Tanner* v *Tanner* in that she has given up the sure protection of a protected tenancy under the Rent Acts, as well as the chance of the leasehold at a low price. If this is the case, the extent of Jill's interest would be commensurate with the terms of the common intention – which could be that she have all the property (subject to repayment to Jack of his money) or some proportion thereof. However, this may be a rather complicated way of looking at the situation and the second angle of approach may be more helpful. Simply, Jack is now seeking to take advantage of the fact that he has an absolute conveyance in his favour and that there is no trust in writing as there should under s53(1)(b) LPA 1925. He is, in essence, attempting to use a statute (s53 LPA) as an instrument of fraud; cf *Rochefaucauld* v *Boustead*. This is established as above viz, the flat was offered to Jill because she was a sitting tenant and at a low price because that tenancy was protected. This is clearly a case for equitable intervention and Jack will hold the flat on constructive trust for Jill, quite possibly as sole owner subject to Jack's right of repayment; cf *Hussey* v *Palmer*.

Question 4

By her will, Celia, after appointing Tug and Tow to be her executors and trustees, left her residuary estate to them upon trust to divide it into two equal parts and to hold such parts upon the following trusts:

a) As to one part, upon trust to pay the income thereof to her husband, Henry, for life upon protective trusts and subject thereto upon trust for such of her children as should attain the age of 25;

b) As to the other part, upon trust in equal shares for such of her children as should be living when her youngest child attains the age of 18.

Celia died last year leaving Henry and three children surviving, Tom, Dick, and Harriet, aged 3, 14 and 21.

Advise Tug and Tow:

i) Whether they may have recourse to the trust income of either fund to pay school fees for Dick;

ii) Whether they may apply trust capital from either fund to enable Harriet to purchase a fast food franchise (a business in which she has five years' experience);

iii) Pending the attainment by Tom of the age of 18, what they should do with the income of fund b);

iv) In the event of Henry's bankruptcy, what they should do with the income of fund a).

Question 4

General comment

Questions on a trustee's power of maintenance or advancement are often difficult and always involve complicated factual situations. They repay careful reading and should be attempted only if you have a clear understanding of the difference between the powers and a sure grasp of the concept of 'intermediate income'.

Skeleton solution

Maintenance – s31 Trustee Act 1925 – protective trusts – prior interests. Advancement– s32 Trustee Act 1925 – meaning of 'benefit'.

Suggested solution

This problem concerns the trustees' powers of maintenance and advancement. The power of maintenance is the power to apply income of a trust fund for the maintenance, education or benefit of an infant beneficiary – the trustees being unable to give the infant his or her share of the income because the infant cannot give a valid receipt. The power of advancement is the power to give a beneficiary part of the capital sum under a trust which he or she would receive (but is not yet entitled to) should he or she fulfil the terms of the trust, eg, reach a specified age. In this case, as there is neither an express power of maintenance or advancement, the trustees' powers arise under s31 and s32 of the Trustee Act 1925. These powers have not been expressly excluded.

i)   *Dick's school fees*

The issue here is whether the trustees may exercise the statutory power of maintenance in Dick's favour by using part of the income from either part of the trust to pay his school fees. Clearly, there is a prima facie chance that the power may be exercisable as Dick is under 18 and he is one of the beneficiaries of both trusts. Again, there is no doubt that the proposed purpose is within s31 TA 1925 as this specifically authorises income to be paid for an infant beneficiary's 'maintenance, education or benefit'. However, the major problem is whether the income arising from Dick's share is actually available for his use. In other words, whether Dick is entitled to the income; sometimes expressed as 'whether the gift or trust carries the intermediate income'.

The income from Part One of the trust is not available to Dick as there is a prior interest – the income is to be paid to Henry under the protective trust (see eg *Re Vesty*). There can be no maintenance from this part.

The income from Part Two may well be available for Dick's maintenance. There is not a deferred gift, but rather a gift contingent on a future event. The gift is therefore either or both (we are not told) a contingent residuary gift of realty and/or personalty. A contingent gift of residuary personalty carries all income earned from the testator's death until the beneficiary actually becomes entitled – *Re Adams*. Further, under s175 of the Law of Property Act 1925, contingent residuary gifts of freehold land (leasehold being personalty for these purposes) will carry the intermediate income. Thus there can be maintenance from this part.

ii) The issue here is whether the trustees may exercise their power of advancement in Harriet's favour. This depends on whether s32 of the Trustee Act is applicable. Advancement is the payment of capital sums to a beneficiary before the time comes when he or she is actually entitled to the fund, although under s32 only half the capital sum due to Harriet can be paid by way of advancement. An immediate problem is whether the proposed use of the capital is for the 'advancement or benefit' of Harriet within s32, for if it is not, the power cannot be exercised. Following *Pilkington* v *IRC*, where a wide definition was given to 'advancement and benefit', it seems likely that the proposed use is within the section, especially since this is intended to be Harriet's career and is not speculative due to her previous experience. The question therefore arises whether the other conditions of s32 are fulfilled. Section 32 enables trustees to advance capital held on trust for any beneficiary (infant or adult), with any interest in the property (contingent, deferred or vested). Thus, the trustee may advance up to one half of the capital from Part Two of the fund to Harriet, even though she may never actually receive an interest (eg because she dies before the youngest child is 18). However, where there are prior interests – as with Henry's life interest under Part One of the fund – the trustees may only advance capital if the person with the prior interest is of full age and gives his written consent s32(1)(c).

iii) Pending the attainment of 18 by Tom, the youngest child, (at which date the trust property can be distributed) s31(2) of the Trustee Act directs that the residue of income from each beneficiary's share not applied for their maintenance while they are a minor should be accumulated by investment during the minority. This becomes available for their future maintenance.

iv) The creation of the trust in Part One of the fund is designed clearly to fall within s33 of the Trustee Act. Under this section, if income is directed to be held on 'protective trusts' for the benefit of any person for their life (as here), then the income is held on the trusts set out in the section. This is simply a shorthand way of establishing an effective protective trust. In the event of a bankruptcy – which would terminate the life interest – the income is to be held on trust for the maintenance, support or benefit of all or any of the following: a) the former life tenant (called the 'principal beneficiary' – Henry) and his spouse and issue OR b) if the principal beneficiary has no spouse or issue, the principal beneficiary and the persons who would be entitled to the capital if the principal beneficiary were dead. All of Henry, Tom, Dick and Harriet are within b) and Henry and possibly the children if they are his issue are within a).

Question 5

By a settlement made by Smith, the trustees, Dum and Dee, were directed to hold a trust fund consisting of shares and debentures in Alpha plc, a public limited company, and certain government stock, on trust to pay the income to Adam for life remainder to his children. The settlement contains no special investment clause except a provision that, before making any change of investment, the trustees should first obtain the consent in writing of Smith.

In 1987, Dum and Dee, with the consent in writing of Smith, sold the shares in Alpha to one of themselves, Dum, for £200,000 (their quoted value) and invested the proceeds in the purchase of shares in Beta plc, another public limited company.

In 1988, Dum and Dee, with the consent in writing of Smith, sold the government stock for £500,000 (its quoted value) and invested the proceeds in the purchase of freehold offices in Docklands.

In 1989, Dum and Dee, without the consent of Smith but with the encouragement of Adam, sold the debentures in Alpha plc for £100,000 (their market value) and invested the proceeds in shares in Delta plc, another public limited company.

The shares in Alpha plc are now worth £300,000; the shares in Beta plc are now worth £100,000; the shares in Delta plc are now worth £200,000 and the freehold offices are worth £250,000.

Advise a) Adam's children, b) Dum and Dee jointly as trustees, and c) Dum individually, as to their respective legal positions.

Suggested Solution to Question 5

General comment
This is a typical question on liability for breach of trust, especially since it involves some consideration of powers of investment. Such questions usually look much harder than they actually are and should be attempted by any candidate with a reasonable knowledge of the law of personal liability of trustees.

Skeleton solution
Personal liability for breach of trusts − standard of care − measure of damages − remedies and defences. Some knowledge of Trustee Investment Act 1961.

Suggested solution
The issues raised in this question concern the individual liabilities of trustees for breach of trust − both collectively and individually − as well as the possible remedies available to a beneficiary whose interest has been adversely affected by such breach. It is, of course, the duty of trustees to invest trust property so that income will be produced for the beneficiaries (eg *Stone* v *Stone*) and trustees will be liable for failing to do so within a reasonable time of the establishment of the trust. This is not the case here. However, trustees may also be liable for breach of trust for investing contrary to their powers of investment or by failing to meet the standard of care required of trustees when dealing with beneficiaries' property. These are the matters in issue here. There are no express powers of investment in this case and therefore, the power of investment is governed by the Trustee Investment Act 1961. It is unlikely that the requirement of Smith's consent excludes the statutory power (if it did there would be no power to invest!), but rather places an additional limit on the trustees in the exercise of the powers under the Act. This means that the trustees cannot exercise the powers of investment under the Act without Smith's consent, but also that Smith's consent cannot make lawful an investment which the Act does not authorise.

Of course, if investment is undertaken (which in this case, if at all must be under the Act), the trust fund must be divided into two equal parts − the narrower range and the wider range part. This is a precondition of the exercise of investment powers under the Act and it is clear that on sale of any of the existing investments of this particular fund, the fund would have to be divided. (NB there is no breach of trust merely by retaining unauthorised investments when the trust was created, because this is not *investment*).

a) The sale of the shares in Alpha to one of the trustees – Dum – and the investment of the proceeds in Beta plc. Adam's children are beneficiaries under the trust and are therefore concerned by the fact that the value of the investment has halved after the sale of Alpha shares and the purchase of Beta shares. However, in order to establish liability for breach of trust – so as to recover the difference in value – they must establish some breach of trust. It is clear that there has been no breach of any express stipulation, for Smith's consent has been obtained. However, there is no indication that the fund has been divided into two halves as required by the Act and, therefore, the investment in Beta shares may be unauthorised. Likewise, there is no indication whether Beta plc fulfils the conditions stipulated in the Trustee Act for investment in public companies (viz not less than £1 million share capital, dividend paid on relevant shares for preceding five years, shares quoted on Stock Exchange, shares fully paid and incorporated in the UK).

Again, trustees investing in wider range investments must obtain and consider advice (s6(2)) as to the suitability of the investment and its suitability in the overall investment profile of the trust. Importantly, however, there is also the general duty of care imposed on trustees when investing trust money. The trustee must act as an ordinary prudent man of business would act if he were minded to make investments on behalf of other people – *Re Whitely*. If any or all of these breaches of trust have occurred, it is clear that both Dum and Dee will be jointly and severally liable to make good the loss to the trust fund, ie the difference between the value of the unauthorised/unwarranted/imprudent investment and the value of the fund before such investment was purchased – *Fry v Fry*. Here, £100,000.

In addition, however, Dum may have incurred further liability as constructive trustee because of his purchase of the trust property. Under the 'self-dealing' rule a trustee must not be both a vendor and purchaser of the trust property and any such sale is voidable at the instance of the beneficiaries within a reasonable time – irrespective of how fair the transaction may have been, *ex parte Lacey*. Smith's consent is irrelevant as it is the beneficiaries' interests that are prejudiced. If Adam's children act within a reasonable time, Dum will be held constructive trustee of the Alpha shares, including their increase in value. It is thus better for the children to pursue this avenue, as they would effectively have an asset worth £300,000, instead of an asset worth £100,000 (Beta shares) plus the £100,000 damages awarded for breach above. If Dum is bankrupt or otherwise unable to meet this constructive trust liability, it may be that Dee could be held liable for his co-trustee's breach of trust either because he was in 'wilful default' within s30 Trustee Act or because he failed in his own duty to supervise Dum.

b) This case is much clearer. A trustee may only invest money in the purchase of land if he is expressly authorised by the trust instrument or by some other statutory provision such as the Settled Land Act, see eg *Re Power*. Neither of these is applicable here and therefore there has been a breach of trust and the trustees are jointly and severally liable for the loss. Smith's consent does not absolve the trustees as, as explained above, the consent is in addition to the requirements of the Trustee Investment Act. It does not replace them.

c) The same general considerations apply to the purchase of Delta shares with the money obtained from the sale of Alpha investments as were relevant in a) above. It is, however, clear that the provisions of the 1961 Act have been breached because the Alpha debentures were Part II narrower range investments and the proposed Delta investments could only be Part III wider range. The income from the sale of narrower range investments should be invested in investments authorised under that Part.

Similarly, Smith's consent has not been obtained and so there is a breach of the clear terms of the trust. Adam's encouragement does not affect his children's ability to sue for breach of trust for any loss sustained, but it would be open to the trustees to plead his instigation as a bar to a claim made by him – eg *Life Association of Scotland* v *Siddall*. Moreover, under s62 Trustee Act 1925, the trustees may seek to impound Adam's beneficial interest to help meet their liability on the ground that Adam instigated or requested a breach of trust with knowledge that he was so doing – *Re Somerset*. This is in effect a form of indemnity for the trustees. They may also try to plead s61 TA, on the grounds that they should be excused liability being (in relation to this breach) honest, reasonable and ought fairly to be excused. This is unlikely given their deliberate disregard of the consent requirement.

Question 6

a) In what circumstances may a trustee be remunerated for his services to the trust?

b) Consider the application of the maxim *delegatus non potest delegare* in the context of a trustee of a personalty settlement who wishes:

   i) to go abroad for a period which may be between six to eighteen months;

   ii) to delegate to a stockbroker the power at his discretion to make changes of investment with a view to producing balanced gains in capital and income;

   iii) in exercise of an express power to revoke the trusts of the settlement and declare other trusts for the benefit of all or any of the same beneficiaries, to vest part of the trust fund in other trustees upon discretionary trusts for the beneficiaries.

Suggested Solution to Question 6

General comment
This is a straightforward question on the law of trustee remuneration and the law of delegation of duties and powers. It is unusual to find these two topics mixed in one question, but such is the trend in recent years.

Skeleton solution
Brady v *Ford* – trustee remuneration – the six exceptions – s25 Trustee Act 1925 – s23 Trustee Act 1925.

Suggested solution
a) It is a fundamental principle of the law of trusts that a trustee must not place himself in a position where his interest and duty conflict – Lord Hershell in *Bray* v *Ford*. One aspect of this principle is the rule that a trustee is in general under a duty to act without remuneration. Trusteeship is essentially gratuitous because the trustee's duty is to effectively administer the trust, but his own self interest would be to gain more personal remuneration by drawing out the time spent on trust work. However, this does not mean that there is anything unlawful in a trustee being paid for his work: rather, it is that such remuneration will not be paid unless the trustee can point to some rule of law or trust provision that authorises such payment for work done. In general, a trustee may be remunerated for his services in the following situations:

  i) Where there is an express remuneration clause in the trust instrument. Although such a clause will receive a strict interpretation (*Re Gee*), such clauses are today common especially where it is the intention that professional trustees (eg a bank) be appointed.

  ii) A trustee may receive remuneration under a contract for services made with a beneficiary. However, the trustee must provide some new consideration for his remuneration as promising to fulfil the trust duties is not enough – he is already obliged to do this.

  iii) There are a number of ad hoc statutory provisions which provide that payment may be made to special kinds of trustee; eg s42 Trustee Act 1925 in respect of corporate trustees and the Judicial Trustee Act 1896.

    iv) A trustee is entitled to keep any remuneration received by virtue of his administering trust assets situated abroad, if such is received without his volition – *Re Northcote's Will Trusts*.

    v) Under the rule in *Craddock* v *Piper* a solicitor trustee is entitled to receive the normal profit-costs for his work done as solicitor to the trust on behalf of himself and his co-trustees in legal proceedings, provided that the costs are not more than would have been incurred by the trust if the solicitor had been acting only for his co-trustees and not himself.

    vi) A trustee may be awarded remuneration under the inherent jurisdiction of the court to ensure the smooth and efficient administration of the trust – *Re Duke of Norfolk's ST*. Remuneration will be ordered if it would be for the benefit of the administration of the trust and can include varying the remuneration actually authorised. The court must consider all factors, but especially the need to protect beneficiaries from unscrupulous trustees.

    In all other cases, a trustee will be called to account as constructive trustee for any payment received by virtue of his position as trustee. He can, however, be reimbursed for expenses – s30(2) Trustee Act 1925 and *Hardoon* v *Belilas*.

b) As a general rule, a trustee cannot delegate his responsibility under the trust for taking decisions. The trustee is in effect a delegate of the settler, and the rule is that a delegate cannot delegate – hence the Latin maxim in the question. To this sweeping statement of principle there are, however, a number of exceptions, all of them designed to facilitate the better administration of the trust.

    i) Under s25 of the Trustee Act 1925 as amended, a trustee may delegate all or any of his powers to another for a period of up to one year, providing that the delegate is not the sole remaining co-trustee (unless a trust corporation). This is essentially a power of attorney and must be granted by written instrument signed by the trustee and witnessed. Written notice must be given to the other trustees. However, the delegation cannot be for longer than a year and if any loss arises through default of the delegate the trustee will be liable as if the default had been his own. All powers may be delegated under s25.

ii) It is an established rule of equity that a trustee can employ an agent to perform certain administrative (ministerial) acts on his behalf. The rule was encapsulated in *Speight* v *Gaunt* where the court held that trustees employing agents in the course of business were not liable for the default of the agent if the employment of that agent was such as would be done by an ordinary prudent man of business. Hence, trustees can employ solicitors, stockbrokers, valuers etc. However, there are some limitations to this rule: notably that the trustee must only employ agents for work within the normal scope of the agent's responsibilities – *Fry* v *Tapson* – and most importantly that only ministerial acts can be delegated under the equitable rules and not the taking of decisions. In this case, if all we had was the old law, then it is probable (but see below) that the stockbroker could not be given the power to make investment decisions, but only the power to carry out the general policy of investment decided by the trustees, ie to act ministerially: cf *Rowland* v *Witherden*. However, according to Maugham J in *Re Vickery*, s23(1) of the Trustee Act has altered this situation by permitting a trustee to employ an agent whether there is any real necessity or not. According to this case, the power to appoint agents in s23 extends to giving those agents the power to take policy decisions in respect of the trust – such as investment decisions. However, this is a controversial view and not widely accepted for it would take away the heart of trusteeship. Such a power is clearly given in s23(2) for certain trust assets abroad and this would indicate that it was not intended to be given under s23(1). Finally, however, perhaps we could argue in our case that in fact this is only a ministerial delegation – not a policy delegation – in that the stockbroker is given power to invest in order to fulfil the overall policy of the trust of achieving a balance between income and capital growth. It is arguable that such a delegation would fall within the narrow view of s23(1).

iii) An aspect of the general rule against delegation already considered is that the person to whom a power is given must in effect exercise that power. A donee of a power cannot delegate the choice involved inherent in that power to another – *Re Morris's Settlement*. In this case, the trustee has been given a power to revoke the trust and declare other trusts for the benefit of all or any of the same beneficiaries. However, in the absence of any express authorisation allowing the trustee to re-appoint the trust property on discretionary trusts, the trustee is not entitled to establish new trustees with discretions as to the choice of beneficiaries. The issue is similar to that decided in *Re Hay* where trustees had power to appoint to such persons or purposes in their discretion except for a limited excluded class. They attempted to use this power to establish themselves as trustees on a discretionary trust for the same object. This was held void as the power demanded an appointment, not a further delegation of the power of choice. A fortiori where the person with the power tries to exercise that power by giving somebody else the discretion.

Question 7

Under the terms of the will of a testator who died in 1983, a fund of £3,000,000 was left to trustees upon trust to distribute the capital amongst such charitable or worthy causes and in such shares as the trustees should in their absolute discretion think fit and the residuary estate was left to the XY Charity. On various dates since the testator's death, the trustees dealt with the fund as follows:

i) £1m was paid to the AB hospital which spent £500,000 on dialysis machines and computer equipment and invested the balance in government stock which is now worth £550,000;

ii) £1m was paid to the CD University which applied the money towards the cost of a new library building. The total cost of the building was £2m;

iii) £1m was paid to the EF Foundation for the Relief of Poverty. It paid this sum into its bank account which at the time was £200,000 in credit. The following day, the EF Foundation drew out £500,000 and applied it in providing hotel accommodation for the homeless. One week later, it received a donation of £500,000 and paid this sum into its account. Since then, further sums have been drawn out and the present credit balance is £400,000.

Advise the XY Charity.

Suggested Solution to Question 7

General comment

For anyone with even a passing knowledge of the law of tracing, this is a good question to answer. It really revolves around *Re Diplock* and the examiner might well think in retrospect that the question was too easy.

Skeleton solution

Tracing – conditions – *Re Diplock* – *Re Oatway* – personal remedies – loss of tracing.

Suggested solution

The issues raised in this question are similar in many respects to those discussed in the landmark decision on the law of equitable tracing – *Re Diplock*. We are asked to advise the XY Charity, obviously with a view to this charity (as residuary legatees) recovering any assets wrongly paid out by the executors. Our first priority is, therefore, to establish that the executors/trustees of the testator have wrongfully distributed the assets subject to the trust. There is no difficulty in this. The trust is expressed to be for 'such charitable or worthy causes' as the trustees think fit. However, in order to be charitable a trust has to be exclusively charitable. As seen in *Chichester Diocesan Fund* v *Simpson* (concerning the will of Caleb Diplock), a trust for 'charitable or benevolent' purposes was held void on the grounds that the trustees could choose objects which were benevolent but not charitable in law. The same is true in our case and the gift is not charitable, not being exclusively devoted thereto. Thus, the trustees have wrongfully distributed the funds. Can the XY Charity recover the property?

The first point to note is that the XY Charity as residuary legatee must sue the trustees personally. They will be liable personally for all the loss, although with such large sums it is unlikely that they could meet this liability in full. Only, however, when they have exhausted this remedy (eg the trustees are bankrupt) may the XY Charity resort to tracing in equity and the *Re Diplock* special in personam remedy.

Equitable tracing

The conditions for the existence of the right to trace in equity were reasonably clearly laid down in *Re Diplock*; there must have been a fiduciary relationship and the plaintiff must have an equitable proprietary interest in the property he or she is seeking to trace. In this case, there clearly is a fiduciary relationship between the XY Charity and the trustees (note the relationship does not have to be between the immediate parties to the action) and as residuary legatees the charity has an equitable interest in the trust. Both the conditions are satisfied.

i)   *The money paid to AB Hospital*
     The hospital has given no consideration for the payment of the £1 million and therefore cannot avoid tracing on the ground of being a bona fide purchaser for value. Of course, if the AB Hospital had notice of the breach of trust, they would be constructive trustee of the property and liable to repay the money in full. Assuming however no notice, they are innocent volunteers. *Re Diplock* makes it clear that if the innocent volunteer has retained the plaintiff's property (more correctly the property in which the plaintiff has a proprietary interest) in recognisable form – even if different from the original form – then the plaintiff may trace to it and recover. Here specific property has been purchased – dialysis machines/computers and government stock. Subject to the general rule that an equitable remedy will not be permitted to do inequity, the XY Charity can recover this property, or in the case of the equipment ask that its monetary equivalent be returned. Further, in the case of the government stock, it appears from *Re Tilley* that the plaintiff may be able to claim the increase in value of the property, ie the extra £50,000. This is because tracing is a right in rem – a right to the thing which is your property irrespective of the value it holds at the moment. Note, however, that *Re Tilley* was decided in the context of an action against a trustee and the court may adopt a more lenient attitude where the tracing is against an innocent third party, especially if that third party has used skill and judgment to increase the value of the property. There is an argument that the profit should be shared: cf *Boardman* v *Phipps*.

ii) Again, prima facie tracing is available. The University again appears to be an innocent volunteer. However, in *Re Diplock*, some of the money had been spent on the alteration of old buildings and the erection of new ones. The Court of Appeal held that in these circumstances no action would lie because it would be inequitable to force an innocent third party to surrender such an asset, especially where the innocent party also contributed substantially to the cost of the property with its own money – as here. Essentially, the plaintiff's property has become untraceable, although this is something of a fiction because if the defendant had been the original trustee it is clear that the plaintiff would have had an enforceable charge over the property as a reflection of its interest (cf *Re Oatway*).

iii) Where an innocent volunteer mixes trust money (ie XY's) in a bank account with his own money – as here – the court in *Re Diplock* decided that a beneficiary did not deserve the special protection afforded by the rule in *Re Hallet* which applied to mixing by trustees. The rule in *Clayton's* case applies so that the money spent on untraceable assets (here the hotel accommodation) is spent on the basis of 'first in first out'. Thus, the first £200,000 of the £500,000 spent on hotel accommodation was EF's own money, the next £300,000 belonged to XY. EF then received £500,000 by donation and the balance in the account stands at £400,000. Under the rule in *Clayton*, this £400,000 must be the remains of the last £500,000 to go into the account (ie last in, last out). It therefore belongs entirely to EF and XY has no claim under tracing to the balance in the account.

In personam

If the personal action against the trustees and equitable tracing fails to secure the return of trust property – as is likely in our case – the XY Charity can fall back on the special in personam remedy of *Re Diplock*. This is a remedy of last resort and it appears to be available only when there has been a wrongful distribution of assets under a will (or possibly a liquidated company – *Re Leslie Engineering*). In effect, it means that although XY cannot receive back its specific property by means of tracing, it can sue the recipients of that property personally for its value. What is more, it is clear from *Re Diplock* that there is no defence of 'change of position' (ie that the money has been innocently spent) to this action and therefore the three charities will be liable. Note, however, that if this action is really a species of unjust enrichment, the case of *Lipkin Gorman* v *Karnaple* may provide some comfort, for in that case the House of Lords has recently held that the defence of 'change of position' is available to an unjust enrichment claim.

Question 8

a) In what circumstances, if any, may the administration of an English trust be transferred abroad (in the sense of the trust fund being invested in overseas investments and the trustees being non-UK residents)?

b) Under the terms of a settlement, investments worth £500,000 are held upon trust to hold the income on protective trusts for Mary during her life and subject thereto for such of her children as attain the age of 21 in equal shares.

Mary is a widow aged 50 and has three children aged 18, 20 and 23. Mary and her children are all agreed that they would like to terminate the trust and divide the investments amongst themselves in agreed shares.

Consider whether this may be done i) without an application to the court, and ii) by making such an application.

Suggested Solution to Question 8

General comment
This is quite a technical question, on the edge of the syllabus and probably would not be attempted by many students. It is quite straightforward in itself and does involve some of the more familiar Variation of Trusts Act problems.

Skeleton solution
Variation of Trusts Act – adult beneficiaries – infant beneficiaries. Meaning of 'benefit' – tax saving – *Re Weston*.

Suggested solution
a) There are various reasons why the trustees of an English trust may wish the investment funds of the trust to be transferred abroad and the management of the trust be placed in the hands of foreign trustees. The most obvious is, of course, that the beneficiaries intend to live in the foreign jurisdiction or, at least, intend to have some real and genuine link with that jurisdiction. It is clear, however, that another important reason why such a move might wish to be made is for the purpose of minimising the tax liability of the trust. This is particularly evident in cases where it is desired to move the investment and administration of the trust to 'off-shore' tax havens, such as the Channel Isles or the Isle of Man.

It is of course perfectly possible for the trust instrument to contain a power authorising the trustees both to invest overseas and, if appropriate, transfer the administration of the trust to foreign trustees. The exercise of such a power may, or may not, be made dependent on the consent of the beneficiaries. Similarly, the appointment of a foreign trustee may be made without any need to have recourse to the court if all the beneficiaries are of full age, sui juris and consent to the changes – as in *Re Whitehead*.

However, in the normal case, it is clear that a trust can only be 'exported' if the terms of the trust can be varied so as to meet the requirements of the foreign law and to authorise the appointment of foreign trustees. All adult beneficiaries who are sui juris can, of course, consent for themselves to such a variation and if they are the only beneficiaries no problem arises. This is, however, unlikely for the trust is likely to include infant beneficiaries or even persons not yet born who will become such beneficiaries – eg future children of the settlor. Such persons cannot consent to a variation as they have no legal capacity and so application must be made to the court under the Variation of Trusts Act 1958 for approval on their behalf.

Under this Act, the court has the power to approve variations on behalf of four classes of persons – persons unborn (eg future children), infants, any person who has a discretionary interest under a protective trust, and any person who would be a member of a class of beneficiaries at a future date, where the class is ascertainable only at a future time. However, in order to be able to approve a variation on behalf of these persons (*except* a person with an interest under a discretionary trust), the court must be satisfied that the proposed variation is for their 'benefit'. This is the most difficult hurdle to overcome when asking for the approval of a variation which transfers the trust property and the administration of the trust abroad.

The most potent and obvious type of benefit is financial benefit and if the tax saving resultant on such a move is substantial then the court would find it difficult to deny that there is 'benefit' within the Act. Similarly, if the beneficiaries are emigrating permanently to a foreign jurisdiction then there may well be an additional intangible benefit in exporting the trust, as in *Re Seal* and *Re Windeatt*. Problems do arise, however, if the link with the foreign jurisdiction is tenuous because it is clear that the court must consider moral and social benefit as well as that which is financial. The leading authority here is *Re Weston* where the Court of Appeal refused consent on behalf of infant beneficiaries to a resettlement of the trusts in Jersey – the object being legitimate tax avoidance. According to the court, 'there are many things in life more worthwhile than money. One of these is to be brought up in this our England, which is still "the envy of less happier lands". I do not believe that it is for the benefit of children to be uprooted from England and transported to another country simply to avoid tax.' There is here, of course, a certain reluctance to approve variations whose sole purpose is tax avoidance ('the avoidance of tax may be lawful, but it is not yet a virtue'), but there is the greater point that the court's responsibility goes beyond fiscal considerations and approval must not be given where such would imperil the 'true welfare' of the children, born or unborn. It is, in essence, that the court must balance fiscal considerations with rather more intangible 'benefits'. Of course, the decision becomes easier if the beneficiaries can demonstrate a genuine link with the new jurisdiction. Finally, we must note that the court has power to order a *variation* of trust – it does not have power to consent to a complete re-settlement on completely new trusts which change the whole 'substratum' of the original scheme – *Re Ball*. This would, of course, depend on the terms of the proposed variation.

i) Under this protective trust, Mary is the life tenant and her children are entitled in remainder. All the children are adult, but not all have obtained vested interests. However, under a protective trust it is difficult for the beneficiaries to effect a variation without recourse to the court. First, the rule in *Saunders* v *Vautier* is inapplicable because not all of the beneficiaries are of full age, sui juris and together absolutely entitled. This is because under a protective trust governed by s33 of the Trustee Act (as this appears to be), when or if the life tenant's interest ends (eg due to an act of bankruptcy), the income is to be paid to the life tenant, his or her spouse and any issue *or* the persons absolutely entitled (the three children). The problem is that a potential and future spouse of Mary would have an interest under the trust – as would any future children – a possibility despite Mary's age. Thus, there are persons with contingent and future interests who would need to consent, but cannot.

ii) Application to the court to vary may be made in a number of ways, although only the last of these is relevant in the circumstances of this case. A court has inherent power to vary the terms of the trust in cases of absolute necessity to preserve the value of trust property eg *Re New*. This is not relevant here. Likewise, the extended jurisdiction to make variations in the administration of the trust which are 'expedient' under s57(1) of the Trustee Act does not assist in this case. Section 57 authorises changes in terms relating to administration of the trust, not changes in beneficial interests. The clearest ground for approaching the court is to gain approval for a variation under the Variation of Trusts Act. As seen above, the court may approve a variation on behalf of incompetent persons and persons who had a discretionary interest under a protective trust. In this case, the court could approve the application on behalf of the unborn children (provided it was satisfied that it was for

55

their benefit) and on behalf of any person who would acquire an interest under the discretionary trusts which would arise if the protective trusts should determine (such as a future spouse) and to this class of persons the requirement of benefit does not apply.

DETAILS FOR DESPATCH OF PUBLICATIONS

Please insert your full name below

Please insert below the style in which you would like the correspondence from the Publisher addressed to you

TITLE Mr, Miss etc.   INITIALS   SURNAME/FAMILY NAME

Address to which study material is to be sent (please ensure someone will be present to accept delivery of your Publications).

POSTAGE & PACKING

You are welcome to purchase study material from the Publisher at 200 Greyhound Road, London W14 9RY, during normal working hours.

If you wish to order by post this may be done direct from the Publisher. Postal charges are as follows:

UK   - Orders over £30: no charge. Orders below £30: £2.50. Single paper (last exam only): 50p
OVERSEAS   - See table below

The Publisher cannot accept responsibility in respect of postal delays or losses in the postal systems.

DESPATCH All cheques must be cleared before material is despatched.

SUMMARY OF ORDER

Date of order:

				£
		Cost of publications ordered:		
		UNITED KINGDOM:		
OVERSEAS:	**TEXTS**		Suggested Solutions (Last exam only)	
	One	Each Extra		
Eire	£4.00	£0.60	£1.00	
European Community	£9.00	£1.00	£1.00	
East Europe & North America	£10.50	£1.00	£1.00	
South East Asia	£12.00	£2.00	£1.50	
Australia/New Zealand	£13.50	£4.00	£1.50	
Other Countries (Africa, India etc)	£13.00	£3.00	£1.50	
			Total cost of order:	

Please ensure that you enclose a cheque or draft payable to **THE HLT GROUP LTD** for the above amount, or charge to ❏ Access ❏ Visa ❏ American Express

Card Number

Expiry Date .... Signature ....

ORDER FORM

LLB PUBLICATIONS	TEXTBOOKS		CASEBOOKS		REVISION WORKBOOKS		SUG. SOL. 1985/90		SUG. SOL. 1991	
	Cost £	£	Cost £	£	Cost £	£	Cost £	£	Cost £	£
Administrative Law	17.95		18.95				9.95		3.00	
Commercial Law Vol I	18.95		18.95				9.95		3.00	
Commercial Law Vol II	17.95		18.95		9.95					
Company Law	18.95		18.95		9.95		9.95		3.00	
Conflict of Laws	16.95		17.95							
Constitutional Law	14.95		16.95		9.95		9.95		3.00	
Contract Law	14.95		16.95		9.95		9.95		3.00	
Conveyancing	17.95		16.95							
Criminal Law	14.95		17.95		9.95		9.95		3.00	
Criminology	16.95						+3.00		3.00	
English Legal System	14.95		12.95				*7.95		3.00	
Equity and Trusts	14.95		16.95		9.95		9.95		3.00	
European Community Law	17.95		18.95		9.95		+3.00		3.00	
Evidence	17.95		17.95		9.95		9.95		3.00	
Family Law	17.95		18.95		9.95		9.95		3.00	
Jurisprudence	14.95				9.95		9.95		3.00	
Labour Law	15.95									
Land Law	14.95		16.95		9.95		9.95		3.00	
Public International Law	18.95		17.95		9.95		9.95		3.00	
Revenue Law	17.95		18.95		9.95		9.95		3.00	
Roman Law	14.95									
Succession	17.95		17.95		9.95		9.95		3.00	
Tort	14.95		16.95		9.95		9.95		3.00	

BAR PUBLICATIONS										
Conflict of Laws	16.95		17.95				†7.95		3.95	
European Community Law & Human Rights	17.95		18.95				†7.95		3.95	
Evidence	17.95		17.95				14.95		3.95	
Family Law	17.95		18.95				14.95		3.95	
General Paper I	19.95		16.95				14.95		3.95	
General Paper II	19.95		16.95				14.95		3.95	
Law of International Trade	17.95		16.95				14.95		3.95	
Practical Conveyancing	17.95		16.95				14.95		3.95	
Procedure	19.95		16.95				14.95		3.95	
Revenue Law	17.95		18.95				14.95		3.95	
Sale of Goods and Credit	17.95		17.95				14.95		3.95	

* 1987–1990 papers only
† 1988–1990 papers only
+ 1990 paper only

HLT PUBLICATIONS

All HLT Publications have two important qualities. First, they are written by specialists, all of whom have direct practical experience of teaching the syllabus. Second, all Textbooks are reviewed and updated each year to reflect new developments and changing trends. They are used widely by students at polytechnics and colleges throughout the United Kingdom and overseas.

A comprehensive range of titles is covered by the following classifications.

- **TEXTBOOKS**
- **CASEBOOKS**
- **SUGGESTED SOLUTIONS**
- **REVISION WORKBOOKS**

The books listed above should be available from your local bookshop. In case of difficulty, however, they can be obtained direct from the publisher using this order form. Telephone, Fax or Telex orders will also be accepted. Quote your Access, Visa or American Express card numbers for priority orders. To order direct from publisher please enter cost of titles you require, fill in despatch details overleaf and send it with your remittance to The HLT Group Ltd.